The Universe is My Home

Leo Greer

BookLeaf
Publishing

Presentation by *BookLeaf Publishing*

Web: www.bookleafpub.com

E-mail: info@bookleafpub.com

ISBN: 9789357441049

First edition 2023

Dedicated to my fine colleagues of the Squad.
You four are entirely and wonderfully to blame
for this book.

ACKNOWLEDGEMENT

First, I must thank BookLeaf Publishing and all of the people working there who helped make this possible. I never expected such an incredible opportunity. Thank you.

I would like to thank my family for the excellent food they fed me and the warm home they supplied while I was writing. The soups, nachos, and chai were greatly appreciated. I am incredibly blessed to have you.

I would finally like to thank myself. It's a bit untraditional, but then again, this whole book is. My hands helped me write, my brain put the words together, and my eyes showed me mistakes in my writing and the good in it. Thanks, me.

PREFACE

Before beginning this book, I would like to acknowledge that the land I am writing in is stolen land. The Indigenous peoples of North America have experienced incredible horrors at the hands of European colonizers, and later, the American government and people, so it is only with great privilege that I write these poems from my home in the northeastern woods of New York. With that understanding, let us move forward.

I have been collecting these poems and editing them for quite a while and I am so excited to share them with you! A lot of my poetry approaches uncomfortable topics such as self-sabotage and grief. I write from experience and understand that these subjects may be triggering to some people. So as a content warning, I would like to let you know that there is some gore, anxiety, depression, and self-sabotage. Please read at your own pace and take care of yourselves.

While unfortunate and sometimes weird, our stories are important to share with the world so as to create greater visibility for everyone's unique situations. The personal is political.

Warmly,
The Poet

a red heart-shaped balloon <3

I have been trying to remember that day
when they lowered you into the ground
and I wonder what was I doing. I know
for certain I was too caught up in
the moment because right now
I know if I were there again
I'd climb right down
those six feet with
you and lay on top
of that box you
were in and
be there
awhile

would
my living
breathing body
of flesh and blood
be strong enough, vibrant
enough, to obstruct your soul's
path from that box to the stars? I don't
know. what would happen next is anyone's
guess. I just think it would be neat to lie down
there with you and search for animals in the
clouds

Sonnet

you aren't a part of Me
any more than I am yours.
I wasn't meant to be
a voice that you ignored.
your first and oldest child
is not a tool or a third parent,
the youngest one is only spoiled
because your charge was errant.
families have been historically glorified,
how could western capitalists say no?
children's rights have been denied;
tongues sharpened on *because i said so.*
I know you've had it rough,
but now enough is fucking enough.

Tummy Ache

can i go home now?
i'm ready for therapy.

Changeling

I do not wish to be lonely,
but it is not the trees,
nor solitude
that makes me so
(for the trees speak to me).
My loneliness is found more often in crowds
or after spending time with busy humans.

Of course, people are nice,
but have you ever spent time in the forest?
(they accept me)
There I cease to be anyone

    but myself.

    And I am whole.

i'm just an underage and sleep-deprived poet taking creative liberties

sometimes I write and
get drunk on
the person I wish I was.

11.07.21

Today was good so I should have known
them feels would creep in on their own.

I did a lot of nothing,
zoned out in my imagination,
unwittingly leaving the door cracked
for that familiar old sensation.

I wandered through my mindscape,
left alone with my thoughts.
I guess I wandered off too far
and now my tears are inky blots.

I let myself be happy,
something I surely deserved,
but my enemy's returned,
She's me, but unperturbed.

She likes to make fun
of how I look in clothes
and notices my discomfort
and hates what I never chose.

Like, that's so uncool, the world already says I'm
not enough,
even though sometimes I'm kind of okay,
but she keeps going through my stuff
and wishing my life away.

Man am I pissed off.
Why is she such a dummkopf?
Can't I just be me?
I really can't be that hard to be.

Some introspection perhaps?

If you don't recognize me, then maybe you should take a look at what exactly was inside you that made you push me away because your face is still familiar, but your heart is a stranger.

Warm regards, me <3

You may be a mystery,
but I no longer feel the need
to solve you.

How could one be so beautiful
and alive
and also cold and empty?
I used to be consumed
by your paradox.

But now I've found
the mystery of myself
is much sweeter.

-L

(sometimes it's a facade and that's okay)

Just because I've
survived so much
doesn't mean I'm
Long-lasting

Yes, my spirit and resolve are eternal
and I am Tough-as-nails, but
Damn.
A few well-placed words and
I'm set back
years of progress.

I support myself, thank you very much

When you ask
why I support some people and their cause,
I have a simple answer:

As a human,
I ask for support-
no, my birth demands it-
and love,
unconditionally.

So when you turn your nose
and ask
why do I support *those people*
I must go
and support myself.

Arts and Sciences Collide

Poetry is a fractal,
spiraling endlessly.
It is greater, by far than 0,
and yet less than 1
(the 1 who reads it)
for the reader is =
to the writer
and both are more complex than the other.

Poetry is irrational.
Fractions...
(by which I mean their interpretations)
fail to capture it entirely,
and yet,
a poem's interpretation is everything.

The sciences cannot exist without wonder.

new pronouns

I don't correct you
when I hear *her* escape your mouth
because I know it's
not your fault
and I know
you want to say the right things
and I'd like you to,
but your realizing that
you made a mistake *again*
might hurt me more
then the mistake itself hurt.

in which Low Self-esteem
meets Ego

I feel like shit.
Nothing's working,
but I think,
"No, you gotta B Positive"

So I look down
at myself:

I feel like shit,
but
Damn, I look good.

Wild Child

Child of the Sun and Stars,
Sister of the Earth,
Brother of the Wilds.

No wonder you
are so confused.

You find acceptance
in your ancestors.
Your lineage is not by blood.

Of nature by birth,
the people might not understand,
but you can,
and that is enough.
You are enough.

Who Am I?

the vegetation lush
Sparse and Rolling
Rich and
Verdant and
vast expanses,
cool shadows peppered with sunshine.
i am many,
not one organism am i.

Life and
Death
Love, Loss, and Rebirth are i.
birds make civilization
of my hair
and flames are my unwitting suitor
-ashes birth our children
and thus life again.

men come:
all the destruction of fire
and none of her forgiveness.
twisted dead children they take from me.
i reach my fingers out to
mother, but
she has been diverted and bottled,

carted off for money,
leaving our warm father, sun.
too grieved, he Burns.

at last, i rejoice.
my mother returned...
hurt, traumatized,
mixed with wind and
Poison.
whipping lashes,
tearing hair,
fauna scattered.
her anger is not meant for me,
i know.
still, i suffer

but i go deeper than
anyone can know.
i am Everything.

I want that "they both live in the end" kind of love.

"I would die for you"
is too plain,
just one of the
average things people have done for centuries
in the entirety of
"I would do anything for you."
I don't want that Romeo-and-Juliet for you.
Do you know what I would do?
I would live.

For you, I would keep breathing
no matter how heavy my lungs are.
I would drink that glass of water
and eat that one more damned apple
because no matter what,
it's important to feed and water myself,
like you say.
Yeah, you're right about that I guess.

For you, I will try
and I'll continue to try
to live for myself and
not for someone else.
I will work on being okay

with self-love
and being enough for me to keep being me.

So yeah,
I'd take a bullet for you,
but that is nothing
and proves as much my weakness of self
as my love of you.
So watch me live
and remember how far I've come.
Just wait and see how much farther I'm going.

love: as played by Decay

The day you told me
I wasn't *good enough*
you tore out my heart.
Arteries severed
with the snapping sound of wet roots and
blood spattered. On the tile floor,
red gems cast aground.
And you ate it-
Fool.
A fool to believe my
love which you
so
envied
could be contained in
one
sole
organ
-and in the HURTING!
In the DEVOURING,
you could somehow transfer it into yourself
-that gaping hole I see
behind your starless eyes.

You were wrong of course,
fool.

Clearly,
though you felt my love
every day
because of our proximity,
you understood none of it-
No. I don't keep it
locked in a chest or
a heart.
It is in my hands,
easy to give and receive.
It has infected my eyes, strengthened
my sturdy legs-
in my blood.
In each CELL.
In my lungs-
it is an endless decay. A fungus.
It is the doom of the modern world,
or rather, its savior.
Even if you kill my heart-
rip it to shreds-
or tear me apart, my love,
it is multiplying
and growing
-expanding.
If you tear apart a rotting log,
you will not stop the rot. Whatever
is eating it from the inside, you've just released.
The spores are taking flight and
my love has taken root.

self-harming doesn't always look the same.

Tearing nails
and chewing lips,
I'm just tired.
Not taking care
of rips and tears
in your skin.
Not letting in
the ones you love,
"forgot" your gloves
(it's cold out there!)
That water's hot
-no it's not,
it's supposed to burn,
let my stomach churn,
forgot to eat,
don't care to sleep,
I'll be ok
this time next week.
I just need You,
I don't care for Me.
Oops, I forgot,
what do I need?
What did I do,
I feel like shit.

No, I'm ok
just let me sit.

Grief is my bitch.

There is a pain in my lungs.
It pulls me down
and it isn't visible
to doctors and machines.

Her name is Grief
and I now know
she will never leave.

She looks for my attention and I am happy to
acquiesce.
She is lonely too,
so instead of denying her,
I think we can be friends.

Winter is.

It is like magic
Like danger and grace
In a symphony
A dance.
Though a hypocrite,
I caution you
Love and admire her
Frosted fingers
Crystalline gown and jewels
But let her not touch
Your warm heart,
Beating with blood
For your veins
Like roots
Are what breathe your life
The forest knows,
Grow roots deep,
The ice may dazzle
Branches above
But keep your heart
Safe and away
Lest it be stolen by fae.

It is Time to Accept Ourselves

lovely child,
you are not a machine.
though the world wants you
to despise yourself,
how can you?
when a flower with the same lines,
the same speckles, and curves,
is so beautiful?

do your scuffed knees not catch you when you
fall?
your crooked toes steady you,
deft arms balancing.
stand tall.
your hands with their bitten nails
will compose marvelous creations.

be gentle with yourself,
flower child,
and let yourself grow wild.
other gardens prune themselves with ferocity
and may tell you to trim your own grasses and
leaves,
but you do not have to be like them.

listen to your body;
the birds fall silent in danger.
let yourself grow,
dance in the wind and rain,
sing!
and paint for no reason
other than enjoyment.

love yourself.

dear child of the earth,
the metals of industry will corrode,
but nature survives
everything.

listen to my words,
sweet whisper-on-the-wind,
hear my secret

    (we are gardens)

* 9 7 8 9 3 5 7 4 4 1 0 4 9 *